Return to Innocence

Poetry of Life, Love, War and the War Within

Michael Morton

Copyright © 2017 Michael Morton

All rights reserved.

ISBN-978-0-692-96007-3

DEDICATION

To my Angels 3
Michelle, Megan and Tristan

CONTENTS

1   Poetry about Life   Pg 1

2   Poetry about Love   Pg 25

3   Poetry about War   Pg 48

1. POETRY OF LIFE

Who's They

They say,
You don't know what you're doing,
You don't know how it's done,
But who's They,

You give all you give,
Cause They make you,
So you will be,
What They want you to be,

They say,
You have too,
Its better this way,
That's what They say,

They say,
You must stay within the lines,
To follow their rules,
Because They said so,

Don't They remember,
Don't They understand,
They were here before,
When They ruled their world,

They try to rule our world now,
They try to be everywhere,
To influence everyone,
But I've had enough of They,

Be who you are now,
Explore your dreams, say what you feel,
They who will mind don't matter,
Those who matter will not mind.

I finished this poem on 9 June 2017. The inspiration for this poem came from hearing the phrase "They say" or "They said". We've all heard this phase most of our lives, but it didn't really hit me until my children would say it over and over again. Everything from their friends to school, it was always "They". What alarmed me about them using this phrase was the way it was limiting their creativity, and ability to try new things. So I began to ask them "Who's They"? The more I would ask, the more we were able to see that "They" weren't always right, and that my children didn't have to be confined to labels or others opinions.

MICHAEL MORTON

Find your Focus

Everything we do in life has a purpose,
There are no random accidents,
Find your focus,
And don't be afraid in life of life,

Your focus begins when you discover your passion,
Let the pursuit of your passion consume you,
Let it give you challenge,
And in that challenge, a sense of meaning,

Sometimes life may get out of focus,
And you just must go on faith,
Trust yourself and your instincts,
Living from this perspective will empower you,

Turn your mirrors into windows,
Get in touch with the song within,
You have a purpose,
A value to all that is life,

When your heart sings in joyous excitement,
And you feel more alive than ever before,
This is the voice of your soul,
Speaking directly to you,

It doesn't matter where you've been,
It only matters where you are,
Sing the song of your hearts calling,
And never let anyone quiet your high,

Organize your life around your passion,
Turn your passion into your story,
Turn your story into your focus,
And in this, you leave your life's legacy.

RETURN TO INNOCENCE

I finished this poem on 29 May 2015. The inspiration for this poem came from talking with a family member who was struggling with direction in life. They were at a cross road in their career, and had to make a decision on which path in life to take. When they asked for some advice, I simply told them "do what makes them happy". It is very easy to get caught up in the haze of life, when you find your passion in life, life will return in focus.

MICHAEL MORTON

Before You Grow

One more time before you grow,
I try to hold on a little bit longer,
One more "I love you",
Before I blink and you're all grown,

Near you I stood to help you stand,
To walk with you hand in hand,
To catch you when you fell,
And pick you up again and again,

Every little thing you do,
Is a big part of me,
From your first little words,
To the day you'll say goodbye,

There was a time,
When my time was only your time,
And together we explored the world,
And in my arms was your favorite place to be,

The butterfly kisses and bedtime stories,
And baby burritos at night,
Dresses for the prom,
And driving lessons that made my knuckles white,

I wonder one day,
If you will recall,
The horseback rides,
And stories I would tell,

Now I don't stand so near,
As I hold back a little tear,
Just one more time before you go,
It has been my life to watch you grow.

RETURN TO INNOCENCE

I finished this poem on 28 July 2016. The inspiration for this poem came from my daughters 18th birthday. Recalling the memories of when she was born, prom and driving lessons. So many special memories I keep in my heart, as she will always be Daddy's little girl.

MICHAEL MORTON

She

She is strong,
She faces her journey with courage and vigor,
And though she may stumble,
Her faith remains complete,

She is a woman determined,
Persevering against the odds,
Refusing to allow hardships,
To dictate who she is,

She feels deeply,
Loves fiercely,
Practical and spiritual,
Her essence a gift unto the world,

Her lips used for truth,
Her voice for kindness,
Her hands for healing,
And her heart for love of all,

She gives the best of herself to everyone,
Determined to never bow her head to wrong,
The tears she cries,
Are as abundant as the laughter she shares,

In her heart,
Lies a spark of heavenly fire,
Dormant in the light of prosperity,
Blazing in the darkness of adversity,

She is strong,
Ennobled by her scars endured,
Her essence a gift unto the world,
And she is you.

I finished this poem on 29 December 2016. The inspiration for this poem came from talking with a co-worker who was going through a divorce. She was always happy and smiling, but that day she was quiet and very reserved. We started talking and she told me how she had been very sad and unsure of herself. This is a very strong woman, beautiful, confident and always caring for others. It really touched me that she was so sad, so I wrote this for her and presented it as a late Christmas gift. It made her smile!

MICHAEL MORTON

What Does Your Heart Say

At the center of your being,
You have the answer,
Only you know who you are,
And you know what you want,

What does your heart tell you,
Why listen to those,
Who are not you,
Who are not living your life,

You cannot live your passion halfway,
You must go all in,
All the doubts in your mind,
Can be answered by the heart,

No one knows your truth,
See things in the now, not as they were or should be,
For the hidden power within your heart,
Is the love of God,

Many fail to discover their path,
A life of purpose,
A life with passion and fulfillment,
Never knowing their compass was always inside,

Your time is limited,
Don't let the noise of other drown your own voice,
Have the courage to listen to your heart,
Don't be trapped by others way of thinking,

The intuitive heart is a gift,
So do not worry about things you cannot know,
When you are in search of your destination,
What does your hear say.

RETURN TO INNOCENCE

I finished this poem on 29 December 2016. The inspiration for this poem came from talking with friends about offering relationship advice. Sometimes it is good to get advice of those closest to us, those we trust. To many times others offer us advice that clouds our thoughts and judgment. Only you know your truth, if you follow your heart you will always find your answer.

MICHAEL MORTON

The Color of Love

If I had to paint a picture,
To show the world what love is,
If I had to create a vision of harmony,
Who could tell me the color of love,

We are all equal,
In the truth that we are different,
We should be united in the reality,
That all colors and cultures were created by God,

We lie if we say we don't see color,
We fool ourselves by not seeing we are equal,
We shine in God's glory because we are different,
We are the same as all God's colors are created in His love,

Mere color,
Unspoiled by meaning or label,
Can speak to the soul,
In a million different ways,

So many see the differences,
But do not respect our similarities,
They are afraid,
Afraid to embrace the beauty of our diversity,

We are destined to grow and learn from one another,
For without each other there can be no prosperity,
There can be no wonder or grandeur,
Without love for all,

In our lives,
We should only see one true color,
The color that provides the meaning of life,
The Color of Love

RETURN TO INNOCENCE

I finished this poem on 28 August 2017. The inspiration for this poem came from seeing all the racial demonstrations and riots on the news. It's sad that we still have people in this world who only see a person's color, instead the person for whom they are. I believe we were all made equal but different. Only when you can see the real person, grow and learn from one another, will you see the color of love.

MICHAEL MORTON

She

She picked us up,
Whenever we fell,
Gave us kisses that always healed,
And quieted our fears in her loving arms,

So many gifts she has given,
None more precious than life,
With a boundless love,
That never ceases to give,

She taught us to believe in ourselves,
All that we are,
All that we will be,
We owe to her,

She has been our compass in life,
Keeping us straight and true,
Walking the path before us,
Showing us the example to follow,

In her heart there is always forgiveness,
Her strength, devotion, and patience,
Ripple throughout our lives,
And our generations to come,

She held our hands for only a short while,
But will always hold our hearts,
With endless hugs,
That remain long after she lets go,

Her loving prayers continue to follow,
Clinging to our lives,
And though we may be far away,
We are never really far from home,

She was and is our greatest teacher,
A teacher of compassion, love and fearlessness,
If love is as sweet as a flower,

RETURN TO INNOCENCE

Then Mothers are the flowers of all that is love.

MICHAEL MORTON

I finished this poem on 7 May 2015. The inspiration for this poem came from Mother's Day. I like to write my own greeting cards and I made this one for a few special mothers I know. Mothers are so very special, and they should be appreciated every day, not just one day out of the year.

The Masculine Heart

He is humble,
His honor the total of his being,
His virtues of life and love,
Are those of the Masculine Heart,

The Masculine Heart is a gift from the Father,
Investing the soul in a timeless purpose,
The reflection of his heart,
Speaks only the truth,

The Masculine Heart is Selfless,
Holding the comfort of others above his own,
Putting more into the world,
Than he takes out,

The Masculine Heart is gentle,
With his hand only raised to protect,
Never using excuses for failure,
Speaking not with waste or lies,

The Masculine Heart is distinguished,
But not complete,
For from the Father he continually seeks,
An ever-growing faith and guidance,

The Masculine Heart knows his worth,
As it is not measured by wealth,
It is in all that is given,
And never from what is gained,

The Masculine Heart knows tenderness,
Respecting the value of all women,
Taking them into his confidence,
And honoring them with dignity and reverence,

Only He that knows the Father,
Can be nurtured by His truth,
For only He that lives the Father's purpose,

MICHAEL MORTON

Shall have the Masculine Heart

RETURN TO INNOCENCE

I finished this poem on 12 January 2016. The inspiration for this poem came from talking with friends about what being a man is really about. Of course we all have our own definitions about what makes a man, but I think it's more important about what's inside his heart, than what he wears or how much money he has.

MICHAEL MORTON

Keep The Faith

You are more than you think you are,
If only you can believe,
It is the spark you keep in your heart,
And the Faith you keep in your life,

Faith is the power to live,
It keeps our hopes and dreams alive,
It is the power to overcome,
The ability to make your dreams reality,

Faith can defeat any injustice,
Faith in faith becomes stronger when tested,
It can move your mountains,
Faith is our foundation and frame of life,

Faith is solid resiliency,
A beginning with no end,
Faith is ever moving,
Growing, guiding as we travel our path in life,

By our Faith we become free,
For the eyes of Faith never tire,
Through the darkest hours,
God's eternal light does shine,

The Faithless will always know fear,
And have no hope to fight,
The Faithless are alone,
The Faithless cannot see tomorrow,

Faith can be regained,
Even after it was lost,
It is the power of your spirit,
That keeps life alive in you,

Hold on to your Faith,
Trust in those who trust in you,

RETURN TO INNOCENCE

Stand in your Faith,
For Faith is the cure,

But Faith can do nothing,
Unless you keep it in your heart,
Unless you believe it,
Unless you are present in life.

MICHAEL MORTON

I finished this poem on 15 November 2015. The inspiration for this poem came from talking with a longtime friend who was going through the most difficult time of his life. He had lost faith in life and the people around him who said they were his friend, but disappeared when he really needed help. We had served in combat together, and though the Army had sent us all over the world, we still referred to each other as brother. I gave him this poem on a day that turned out to be his most difficult day, and with a little faith and a lot of prayers he and his family made it through. Faith will see you through your hardships, but only if you are present in life to believe it.

Burdens

Hate is learned,
Not a burden imposed at birth,
The gravest threat to mankind,
Is the extreme of hatred for minimal reason,

Hatred learned is engraved upon the heart,
To let go of these burdens,
You must unlearn what was learned,
You must let go of what imprisons your heart,

These burdens obscure the truth,
And the truth is,
Unless you let go of these burdens,
You will never move forward in life,

Hatred is a refuge for the unaware,
Its only purpose is to divide and destroy,
It is the enemy of freedom,
The adversary to all mankind,

The suffering imposed by others,
To degrade the life of any man,
Demeans the lives of all man,
Even our own,

The hardest thing in life,
Is letting go of what you believed was real,
Make your burdens part of your history,
Not your destiny,

The only person who can surrender your burdens,
Is you,
For you cannot live in the present,
If you are weighed by burdens of the past.

MICHAEL MORTON

I finished this poem on 25 May 2017. The inspiration for this poem came from trying to understand racism and how it continues to evolve in our country. Hatred is learned, it's not something we are born with. I use the term burden to describe racism, as I believe that hatred will only weigh you down in life. Hatred will blind you from the truth, and limit your ability to grow as person in the world. The sad thing about racism, it is continually spread around the world like a deadly disease.

2 POETRY OF LOVE

Butterflies

When I think about her,
I get butterflies in my stomach,
She is all I've ever wanted,
There is nothing about her I would ever want to change,

She looks at me,
With a light in her eyes I've never seen before,
I look at her,
And see everything I've been looking for,

I can speak to her without fear,
We can talk about anything,
Or nothing at all,
And I'm still happy just to be with her,

The moments when I miss her,
I re-rea d her messages in silence,
My heart begins to race,
And I smile like a little school boy,

Every moment when I am away from her,
I grow homesick for her touch,
Her smile alone can make my day,
And I tell all my friends "That's Her",

I love to hold her close just to hear her heart beat,
I stay awake just to watch her sleep,
She is my world,
And worthy of all my being,

When I think about her,
I get butterflies in my stomach,
The only thing I would want to change of her,
Is her last name.

RETURN TO INNOCENCE

I finished this poem on 15 September 2017. The inspiration for this poem came from hearing a woman on the radio talk about how she still gets butterflies every time she meets her boyfriend for a date. I took that thought and wrote this poem. I put my own thoughts and feelings into this poem, as this what I would love to have in my life again.

MICHAEL MORTON

A Summer Young

In starry silence,
Treasured memories I hold in my heart,
Reminiscences of a Summer long ago,
Memories of a Summer Young,

She was an Angel,
With a heart of gold and Stardust smile,
The source of many misty-eyed sunlight smiles,
The song of Nightingales unto my heart,

We stayed up all night long,
Hungry for life and love,
The slow waves flowing over the sandy shore,
The soft moonlight caressing her eyes,

A top the world our first kiss,
The ocean breeze warm against our skin,
Entwined in true loves embrace,
A love story daring and true,

In every boys life there is a girl,
A girl he will never forget,
A storm that rages within his heart,
And a summer where it all began,

These are the days I dream about,
Days when I see the stars kiss the moon,
When I smell the ocean,
Days when the summer breezes blow,

When I remember a Summer,
It will always be this one,
The summer when I found my heart,
My Summer Young

I finished this poem on 15 August 2017. The inspiration for this poem came from a very special time in my life as a young man, when I found my first true love. I was 19 at the time, and stationed at Guantanamo Bay, Cuba as a Marine. Her sister was in the Navy, and stationed there as well. The night we met, I fell so hard for her. We spent the next week or so together as much as we could. I don't remember all the time we shared, call it age or the Traumatic Brain Injury (TBI) I got in combat, but I do remember being so madly in love with her. She had to leave Cuba and go back to start college. We kept in touch via letters and phone calls, and visited when we could over the next year or so. Although we never ended up together, she made a special impact on my life. A summer I will never forget.

MICHAEL MORTON

Another Brick

So many stones I've been given,
As the wall grows bigger each time,
Each brick made of fear and heartache,
With pain and failures deep ingrained,

I sit atop the tallest tower,
My thoughts obscure and dark,
Brick by brick,
I guard my source,

My laughter gone,
My eyes filled with tears yet to fall,
I will not show you inside,
The only way to survive this reality,

Higher and higher,
Strengthening day by day,
Living in a state of numbness,
Empty,

Another brick in the wall,
To keep the waves from crashing down,
A sanctuary from crippling pain,
With roots that cannot be broken,

I cannot be reached,
Nor can I reach out,
Protected by thick colorless stones of isolation,
Sealed by the tears of sorrow and sadness,

Another brick in the wall,
To protect what's left inside,
A retreat to keep me in,
And everyone out.

I finished this poem on 21 July 2017. The inspiration for this poem came from thinking about love and heartbreak. Over the many years of heartache and disappointment, you tend to build a wall around your heart. Every heartache you receive, you add another brick to the wall. Some bricks are bigger than others, and tears seal the wall ever stronger. The wall is a sanctuary from the pain, and you cannot come inside. The wall keeps you safe within, but it also keeps everyone out.

MICHAEL MORTON

Gaze Upon The Moon

In the silence of the night,
I see the stars shine above,
From the window of my heart,
I gaze upon the moon,

I find myself trapped in seclusion,
With vivid dreams of empty illusions,
Broken by the yearning of loneliness,
Hoping someday to be found,

No one knows the depth of love,
Until it leaves you all alone,
You feel the ghosts of their lips,
As hope flies away on the wings of time,

Only the ashes remain,
Of what was once my fire,
So much of me is missing,
Sorrow begins to rust my soul,

Stormy tears fall from my eyes,
As I dwell on memories past,
Searching in the weeping rain,
Searching for the half that makes me whole,

This hole in my heart,
I walk around it every day,
And when the night comes,
I fall in again and again,

Each night I gaze into the heavens,
Praying for my heart to heal,
I try not to cry,
For my tears will hide the moon.

RETURN TO INNOCENCE

I finished this poem on 12 June 2017. The inspiration for this poem came from sitting on my back deck by the hot tub, and gazing up at the moon. I was thinking about someone very special that was no longer in my life, and how we would spend time together just being together. Life is meant to be shared, so find that someone you can gaze upon the moon with.

MICHAEL MORTON

The Joy I See

The Joy I See,
A life of new beginnings,
Only from the heart,
Can a river of joy flow like this,

The Joy I see,
The rest of life starting now,
A bliss kept from here to eternity,
Two souls joined for life,

The Joy I see,
The happiness within their eyes,
Full of life and wonder,
Is shared with me in a smile,

The Joy I see,
The beating heart of life,
A connection to everything beautiful,
The infallible sign of the presence of God,

The Joy I see,
The source of their smile,
The expression of love in movement,
The sheer surging of life in a moment,

The Joy I see,
A life nurtured and endeavored to live,
Like walking under a sun filled sky,
Every moment a memory to kept,

Its moments like this,
I am reminded of the gifts we have in life,
That there is hope yet for me,
In the Joy I see.

I finished this poem on 31 July 2017. The inspiration for this poem came from watching a music video of the song "Sugar" by the band Maroon 5. In the video, the band travels around Los Angeles surprising new weds by performing at the wedding reception. The joy you see in the couples eyes, you can tell they are so happy in love. The joy I see in their eyes is the joy I hope to find in my life one day.

Mr. Nice Guy

Nice Guys always finish last,
Placing others before themselves,
Sharing their vulnerabilities,
Their gentleness mistaken for weakness,

Challenges,
They are not,
The challenge of the chase,
There is no appeal,

Placed upon a pedestal,
Labeled as desperation,
Unconditional respect,
Branded as cowardly,

She says one thing,
But pursues another,
Attracted by their emotionless charm,
And predatory nature,

Mr. Nice Guy will always be there,
But always in the "Friend Zone",
Hoping she will see,
Hoping for the change that never comes,

Mr. Nice Guy listens,
And will always keep her secrets,
In his true self,
She is treasured,

Nice Guys will always finish last,
For there is no wonder in the chase,
Yeah he's that guy,
The one who's never an option.

I finished this poem on 12 June 2017. The inspiration for this poem came from me, as I am Mr. Nice Guy. I was raised to be a gentleman, to respect women with respect and dignity. I was taught to treat all women like a lady, and my lady like a Queen. It took me a few years after my divorce before I considered dating again. Divorce is not an easy thing to recover from. I have high standards and will not compromise my values just to be with someone, so finding someone wasn't easy. The ladies I met were lovely and intelligent, and said they were looking to find a gentleman. Unfortunately, they went back to the old boyfriends who were said to be abusive and disrespectful. I don't know how many times I have heard "you are such a nice guy", "such a gentleman", "but"! Relationships take two, so I am at fault as well. But no matter how long it takes, I will not change my heart, I will always be a gentleman.

MICHAEL MORTON

Something So Strong

Something So Strong,
It cannot be articulated or explained,
It makes you powerful,
Determined beyond all belief,

The coward says there is no such thing,
As they hid in the shadows of its existence,
Their spirit ever so small,
Because they are too small to believe,

Something so strong,
If you let it come into your life,
It will see the most negative parts of you,
And still never leave,

Something so strong,
It can break down all walls,
Defeat all misery,
And send you soaring above the clouds,

Something so strong,
It enwraps over very nature,
It can endure any circumstance,
And reach across any distance,

Something so strong,
There is no greater inspiration,
It defies the rules of reason,
With the magic to change your world,

Something so strong,
In it nothing is impossible,
It has the power to see all people,
It is the source that touches the soul.

RETURN TO INNOCENCE

I finished this poem on 29 August 2017. The inspiration for this poem is simple LOVE.

MICHAEL MORTON

The Untold Truth

My smile hides the sadness,
My laugh hides the pain,
Things are not as they seem,
And I am tired of pretending,

I walk in this world all alone,
A lost soul out of place,
With a heavy head,
And empty heart,

I want so badly to catch my breath,
To hold tight to something other than a dream,
To wake and feel alive,
No more silence for companionship,

The darkness clouds my mind,
Wishing I could just see,
The Untold Truth echo's from my heart,
And I try so hard to ignore it,

Maybe they are right,
Maybe I get my hopes up too high,
When everyone around me seems so happy,
And I just want the same,

I am tired of feeling sad and empty,
Tired of dreaming the dream,
Tired of wondering why,
Why not me,

What if there's someone who thinks about you when they can't sleep,
And smiles at the thought of your name,
Someone who would make you their whole world,
And you're just too busy to see them.

I finished this poem on 27 April 2015. The inspiration for this poem came from seeing so many couples together, and I was alone. It made we wonder, why not me. You pretend you're okay, and life is good. But that is a hard mask to wear. So many times I would get my hopes up, only to be let down again and again. But you cannot give up hope; your one is out there. Just don't be too busy not to see them.

MICHAEL MORTON

Speaking In Love

How does true love speak,
In the embrace where sadness melts,
In the joy of a kiss,
From the lips of a tender heart,

Deep within the fire,
That flows through tender veins,
In the shyness of hands,
That thrill and tremble with a touch,

Love makes no demands,
As love is always spoken freely,
In the search to find one's meaning,
Love is at the heart of our existence,

Loves languages do not erase the past,
But make the future possible,
Love is a choice,
A choice only you can make,

When love is spoken true,
Mountains can be moved,
The roughest seas can be crossed,
And the greatest hardships endured,

When speaking in love,
We speak that of our own,
When speaking in the love of another,
Love expressed in theirs can mean the world,

We all blossom,
When speaking in the languages of love,
It's when we are spoken to in our own,
That we speak with true love.

I finished this poem on 18 May 2015. The inspiration for this poem came from talking with a friend about the languages of love. The topic comes from a book 5 Love Languages. We all communicate differently, and learning to speaking in your partner's language will express your love in a way they understand and appreciate.

MICHAEL MORTON

Treasure

The One you should treasure,
But she is not your possession,
She should be loved,
And never a heavy hand upon her,

She is yours to treasure,
Her value greater than all the worlds gold,
Be proud to have her on your arm,
And show the world she is yours,

She should always be built up,
And never torn down,
By the words you speak,
Or the silence you impose,

She should be embraced every day,
With the warmth of your loving arms,
Never pushed away,
Even when your day was long,

Words spoken in anger,
Will hurt her fragile heart,
Never a target of your frustration,
She deserves so much more,

She should be admired for her love,
And looked upon as a gift from above,
Appreciate her commitment to you,
And return her commitment with your own,

Simply lover her every moment of everyday,
With all that you possibly can,
Treat her as your greatest treasure,
And lover her each day as if it were your last.

I finished this poem on 4 May 2015. The inspiration for this poem is simple. You should treasure your woman above everything in life but the Father. For she is a gift from the Father, and the greatest treasure you will ever have.

MICHAEL MORTON

Over Again

I want to go back in time,
And love you all over again,
Back to our first embrace,
And taste our first kiss,

Heart to heart,
Soul to soul,
Over and over again,
I fall for you,

There are moments,
When it's like I see you for the very first time,
And the times we are apart,
My heart grows fonder,

Because every time I look at you,
I am right back where I began,
Falling your love,
All over again,

All that was,
And all that will ever be,
You are my one,
My one and only one,

I love you more than you'll ever know,
You are the inspiration in my life,
The smile within my soul,
The love that gives me faith to believe,

In your love my heart has found its home,
In your arms I find my comfort,
In your smile I find my peace,
You are my today, my tomorrow, and my forever,
Over and over again.

RETURN TO INNOCENCE

I finished this poem on 4 May 2015. The inspiration for this poem is another simple one, Love. This is how I believe love should be.

3 POETRY OF WAR

Return To Innocence

Your darkness does exist,
You must recognize it,
But only as you focus on remembering the good,
In your journey to return to innocence,

A return to Innocence signifies,
We have faith in ourselves and others,
It allows us to be vulnerable,
And open without fear,

When you return to Innocence,
You will find your source of inner strength,
An inherent wisdom and healing,
A new life is waiting for you to take the first step,

The eyes of truth are always watching,
The past and future are only in your imagination,
The present moment,
Is the only one that never ends,

It takes courage to question yourself,
You will never find the light with your eyes closed,
You will never find your peace,
By dwelling on your mistakes,

Just look inside your heart,
Don't be afraid to be exposed,
Don't let pride,
Build a prison from which there is no escape,

Give thanks for every moment,
Every breath, every fault,
Every laugh, every sigh,
Every chance is a new chance in life,

The beginning of your tomorrow starts today,
Every step is a step forward,

MICHAEL MORTON

Don't let pride keep your words,
Embrace humility and admit when you need help,

Return to innocence and see the world in everything around you,
The beauty of a rainy day,
Hold endlessness in your heart,
And an eternity of love for all.

RETURN TO INNOCENCE

I finished this poem on 21 May 2015. The inspiration for this poem came from talking with Veterans, and their recognizing they have PTSD. Finding peace from PTSD is a journey, a journey to find your true self. The innocence that was you before war.

MICHAEL MORTON

Behind the Stone

Behind the Stone of polished black,
A clouded reflection of war long forgotten,
Row upon row, names of the departed are etched for all time,
A black scar rising upon the history of man,

Behind the Stone,
Many a life will never be known,
Dreams cut short by the delusion of man,
Dreams that remain sealed forever,

Behind the Stone,
Faces look out at the faces looking in,
Both faces searching for hope,
Watching, waiting to be remembered,

Behind the Stone.
Cracks form by the tears of many,
Those in front attempt to mend the wounds,
Placing symbols of healing within the fractured blackness,

Masses gather to the Stone,
To touch once again their memories of a different time,
Tears are laid upon those names read and remembered,
But many yet will go unspoken,

Behind the Stone,
The dead have seen the end of war,
Those that face the polished black,
Have been dying since coming home,

The Stone of polished black is not a memorial of war,
But a memorial to life,
For the Stone remembers their names,
And the Stone never forgets.

RETURN TO INNOCENCE

I finished this poem on 21 May 2015. The inspiration for this poem came from talking with a support group of Vietnam Veterans. They were having a Vietnam Veterans reunion and I was asked to write a poem for them. I used the Vietnam War Memorial (The Wall), as a symbol to highlight the sacrifices our Vietnam Veterans made for our freedom.

MICHAEL MORTON

Open Your Eyes

Leaving without a sound,
Not even a chance to say why,
Engulfed by the darkness,
Only you could have seen,

Now a single rose I lay,
As the tears fall from my face,
It's a cold day to say goodbye,
If only you could have seen,

A permanent solution,
To a temporary problem,
You were laid to rest,
As we are left holding on to yesterday,

Open your eyes,
See the world and your tomorrow,
Your candle has been lite,
Its ok to leave the pain behind,

Stand up,
No need to drown in the past,
No need to wander in the dark,
There is no solution on the other side,

Take my hand,
I will keep you clear and calm,
A lifetime of possibilities,
Waits in front of you,

This can be the first day of your life,
To find the peace you need to find,
You have the power to heal your wounded heart,
Just Open Your Eyes

RETURN TO INNOCENCE

I finished this poem on 21 May 2015. The inspiration for this poem came from hearing another Veteran had committed suicide, as they were struggling with PTSD. I have lost a few brothers to this horrible tragedy. Those who are suffering with PTSD are wandering around in the dark. A darkness you cannot see. They need help to see there is a tomorrow, that they can leave the pain behind. If they open their eyes, get them to see they need help and they get it, they can find the first day of their new life. Suicide is a permanent solution to a temporary problem.

MICHAEL MORTON

The Disease

In thunderous silences,
The Disease does sound its trumpet,
Echoing through the veins,
Of those who hear its call,

The disease does not value life,
It feeds on the decay of the soul,
Only life can value life,
And only life can see its truth,

On hollowed breath,
The Disease speaks against the grains of truth,
Which settle on the tongue,
Siphoning the meaning from melting hearts,

Shrouding the heart in obscurity,
Destroying the tenets structure within,
Engulfing the reason,
With walls of hopelessness,

The innocent see no more,
The Disease will not perceive the certainty,
Nor hear the whisper of care,
Over the lullaby symphony playing in silent,

Hearts fil with sadness,
As the lie tells another lie,
Warping and twisting the conviction,
Taking what is not to be taken,

Do not let it in,
Do not listen to the lies it tells,
Find in you the reason to be found,
And shed the light on all the ones who never thought they could see.

RETURN TO INNOCENCE

I finished this poem on 9 September 2015. The inspiration for this poem came from talking with some combat veterans about the rising numbers of suicides. Suicide is a disease that imprisons the soul. It builds a wall around your heart, and engulfs you into darkness. The current suicide rate amongst veterans today (September 2017) is an average of 22 per day. Suicide is a lie, it tells you everything will be better, the pain will go away. But the truth is, those that commit suicide pass their pain onto their family and friends. They are left holding on to the victim's tomorrows, with an eternity of empty answers.

MICHAEL MORTON

The Crucible

The Crucible,
The test of tests,
Once you've started,
Never will it end,

The erosion of creation,
The destroyer of the dream that is peace,
The blood stained world,
Forever weeps in ferocious silence,

Forged in the Crucible,
Are a Brothers bond,
Brothers in Arms,
A bond that will see no end,

Mourning the loss of One,
Is a heartache like no other,
A pain that reaches the soul,
An infinite stain of sorrow,

The Crucible invades your dreams,
A living hell of nightmares,
The screams of the fallen,
The faces that never look away,

The distant cries of the innocent,
Echo throughout all time,
As the days ever so hopelessly drift away,
The unforgiving lies spread upon the winds,

The Crucible will forever change you,
Deep within your core,
Causing the strongest,
To live with fear and regret,

The Crucible is now,
It is everywhere and forever,

RETURN TO INNOCENCE

Look no further than your mind,
For the shadows of the test have consumed you.

I finished this poem on 24 March 2015. The inspiration for this poem came from talking with combat Veterans about war. War is only about death. Those that have been to war, will forever be bonded together. War changes you forever, and many times it's not for the good. These changes do not go away. You must find a way out of the darkness, make friends with the faces in your dreams and ask for help. Seeking help is not a sign of weakness my brothers and sisters. I did!

Lifeless Eyes

Into those eyes,
Lifeless and dark,
No truth, no lies,
Only tormented years of numbing pain,

They see into nothingness,
Bended,
Drained,
Enslaved,

A mind trapped inside the trauma,
Here, but still there,
Searching for an open door,
Looking for a tomorrow without fear,

So many images absorbed,
A mind mazed with mirrored walls,
Trapped within a silent prison,
Into a purple haze of nothingness,

Noises replay the frightening scenes,
As haunting cries engulf the body,
All that is hell,
There is no escape,

Hardened of heart,
Confined within the fury,
Drowning in memories,
Buried deep within the soul,

Behind those lifeless eyes,
A broken life and shattered mind,
Tears fall from untold scars,
As darkness suffocates the broken truth

I finished this poem on 19 June 2017. The inspiration for this poem came from visiting with some combat veterans during a Wounded Warrior event. I could tell one of the Veterans was really having a hard time with the crowd and loud noise. He never said a word, but his eyes spoke volumes. He was there, but he really wasn't there. Only because I have been there, could I recognize his trauma. PTSD is wound you cannot see, and it cannot be fixed by a few simple counseling sessions. That would be like trying to dam Niagara Falls with a Solo cup. The healing from PTSD takes time, and it cannot be measured by a calendar. If you have never served in the military or been to combat, you may not understand the complexity of what they are going through. If you know someone who is struggling with PTSD, the best advice I can offer is to just simply tell them you care, and you are there to listen. They may open up to you or they may not. But they will hear you.

Sidelines

So you think you're on the sidelines,
Watching all that is life go by,
Placed there by your unique challenges,
Confined only by your consciousness,

You think you've lost everything,
But you have so much more,
In your heart lies the spark,
In your soul burns the will,

Your challenges are a gift,
A gift that makes you strong enough to overcome it,
Smart enough to figure it out,
And brave enough to use it,

You can endure overwhelming obstacles,
If your belief becomes your conviction,
Obstacles are placed in our paths not to stop us,
But to ignite our strength and courage,

Don't confine your spirit,
Even if you only do one thing well,
You are needed by others,
More than you know,

The journey starts with one belief,
By doing what is necessary,
By doing what is possible,
And soon you are doing the impossible,

The human spirit is one of ability,
Resiliency and courage that no challenge can steal away,
Face the Sunshine,
And your shadows will fall behind.

I finished this poem on 25 May 2017. The inspiration for this poem came from hearing combat Veterans talk about their disabilities. Some of these Veterans have lost limbs, sight, or some with wounds you cannot see. Small minorities of Veterans with these disabilities hide behind them, or use them as an excuse to not move forward in life. The truth is, the only limitations you have are the ones you place upon yourself. During one of my combat tours in Iraq, we hit an IED (Roadside bomb) and it destroyed our HUMMV. We all sustained injuries, but the driver of the truck ended up losing both his legs due to being badly burned. I struggled with the guilt of being the leader and not being able to save him. I was hurt badly, my back and neck, but was able to walk and move around. I felt sorry for myself, and yet he was hurt far worse than I was. He received great treatment at the Army hospital in San Antonio, and I was told many times that he was up and moving around in a wheelchair. Going to visit other wounded veterans, motivating them to get up and start moving. He refused to sit on the sidelines; he was alive, and going to be alive in life. That's when I stood up and said no more! I am going to sit on the sidelines, and watch life go by.

War In Peace

I yearned so long,
To finally make it home,
My duty done,
To find my peace from war,

I thought my war had ended,
But my eyes tell a different tale,

I see into nothingness,
My mind bended,
My peace enslaved,
My nightmare begun,

Fires rage,
Screams of pain,
Cries for help,
The smell of death surrounds me,

I can see their faces,
The dead and wounded,
Those heroes known,
And those I didn't,

I fight to succumb,
My mind drained dry,
The pestilence fear overwhelming,

Prayers for deliverance I try,
Senseless numbing no resolve,
My fate uncertain,
My destiny unknown,

As long as the war is alive in me,
My wounds do not heal,
No peace I find,

Hear me,

MICHAEL MORTON

My family and comrades,
This fate I have assigned,

To find peace,
Peace for us,
And those like us,

Death is a fact of War,
And wounds will heal in time,
But no one returns unwounded,

I finished this poem on 24 April 2015. The inspiration for this poem came from talking with fellow students in my Master's program at the time. The subject obviously was PTSD, and the difficulties that veterans have expressing their thoughts and feelings about their experiences. So I wrote this from the Veterans perspective, my perspective at one time. Those that have been to war, want peace more than anything else in their lives, and that peace can come in many different forms. Some will use alcohol or drugs to find it; others will simply shut the world out completely. We all have our own way of dealing with it. Not everyone who has been to war, was in combat. Not everyone had to take a life, or see lives taken in front of them. One thing about war is for sure, no one returns unwounded.

MICHAEL MORTON

You

The waves are crashing over me,
Pulling me ever so down,
I fight and struggle to survive,
But You don't see anything wrong,

You don't see me looking for the danger areas,
Where the enemy will hide,
How I enter the room,
The hazards along the roads,

Faces from the past come back,
The smells,
The voices,
The heat from which there is no escape,

Sleep is no comfort,
Cause I don't really sleep,
I don't want to see this anymore,
And yet I can't get it out of my head,

Who are You to judge me,
You don't know what I have been through,
You don't know how I feel,
And yet You sit there with a smile on your face,

To hell with you,
Your reality is not my reality,
I am trained to show no weakness,
I don't deserve your condescending attitude,

I pray for a little bit of normalcy,
To find a few moments of peace,
Just to catch my breath,
To feel good again,

You say I look fine,
This struggle within you cannot begin to understand,

RETURN TO INNOCENCE

PTSD is my war,
War is my reality.

I finished this poem on 24 April 2015. The inspiration for this poem came from watching a news article on PTSD, and the horrible treatment of Veterans with PTSD. YOU CANNOT SEE PTSD!!!!!! But it's there. The treatment of combat veterans and how they are judged is despicable. I am sorry if people find this offensive, but your reality is not theirs. Unless you have been through the horrors yourself, how can you judge what you don't know? You cannot come home from a year or more of death and destruction and just turn it off. You will still be in a hyper vigilant state of alertness. You have been trained to see the danger areas, and you see them. During my combat tours I averaged about 4 hours of sleep a day, but you really don't sleep. When you come home from war, you are exhausted. You sleep, but you really don't get restful sleep for many years. We all try to find peace, to catch our breath from the marathon that is war. Just because we may look normal, doesn't mean there isn't a war raging within.

My War

I love to watch the sunsets,
And listen to the birds on high,
The laughter of my children,
But I miss my war

War is exciting,
A continuous moment in awe,
Where your senses come alive,
In a serene state of excitement,

The sounds of war,
Soldiers laughing,
The roar of gunfire,
The silence of the soul,

I am home now, safe,
But feel foreign,
Like a stranger in a familiar dream,
A Deja vu that should not be,

Dreams in horror haunt my mind,
The images sicken me,
But their familiarity pulls me in,
A painful comfort of peace,

Some are memories best forgotten,
Others I want to remember,
To live through it again,
To feel the edge one more time,

But I feel hollow inside,
As the tremors ever linger,
Like being in a terrible storm,
Both powerful and helpless,

I am hungry for it,
Thirsting for that feeling,

MICHAEL MORTON

The edge,
Where control and chaos co-exist,
And yet I hate it,
The death and destruction,
The senseless loss of life,
The rage of violence that was always close,

A place where death is ever present,
And it doesn't really matter,
I miss the high,
I desire the unknown,

Only those who have been,
Know the darkness of war,
The never-ending emptiness,
The thrill that only it can be,

There is no freedom after war,
Only a lonely burden of guilt to carry,
But you crave it,
The death and rebirth of your soul,

The war has twisted my path in life,
Light is dark, dark is light,
For better or worse,
I see the world differently,

I can see the comfort in my family's eyes,
I am home, safe,
Life continues with no uncertainty,
But I miss my war.

I finished this poem on 28 March 2014. The inspiration for this poem came from talking with my fellow comrades of whom we served in combat together. Even though we despise war, we miss it. We don't miss the death and destruction; we miss the high of adrenalin. We miss the bonds made with men you will never forget. We miss living on the edge, in a place where control and chaos exist together. Imagine being a 19 year old young man, deployed to combat with the power of life or death in your hands. At 19 you are in charge of 6 other young men, and you are responsible for their lives and millions of dollars of worth of military equipment. You spend a year or more training for war, then a year or more at war. The entire time you eat together, you live together, and you fight side by side. You become closer to these men than you are to your families. When you return from a combat tour, many Soldiers leave the military, while some move on to another duty station. You see the world differently, and for better or worse, you will miss it.

ABOUT THE AUTHOR

Michael Morton is a freelance writer and Poet. He has work forthcoming in Leadership, Poetry about PTSD, Inspirational Poetry and *Life Lessons for Little People*, children's stories that promote values and morals . He is retired from the U.S. Army and served numerous combat tours in Iraq and Afghanistan. You can visit his website at
www.angelsthreeproductions.com

www.ingramcontent.com/pod-product-compliance
Lightning Source LLC
Chambersburg PA
CBHW061340040426
42444CB00011B/3014